Hairstyle

Fashion

Coloring Books for Adults

Flowers and Doodles Patterns Designs for Relaxation and Mindfuness

COLOR TEST PAGE

TEST YOUR COLOR

www.ingramcontent.com/pod-product-compliance
Lightning Source LLC
Chambersburg PA
CBHW081536280526
45788CB00010B/3253
* 9 7 8 1 5 4 4 2 0 9 6 1 6 *